PIERRE TEILHARD DE CHARDIN was one of the most remarkable men of our century. Born to a distinguished French family in 1881, Teilhard heard and heeded a divine call to the priesthood. A member of the Jesuit order, he also became a noted paleontologist. Teilhard was a whole man; his theological training, scientific knowledge and mystical sensibility were not to be compartmentalized. It was such a mind that reflected in a new way on the meaning of human existence, bridging the traditional chasm between religion and science. His books THE PHENOMENON OF MAN (1941) and THE DIVINE MILIEU (1927), published only after his death in 1955, probe deeply into the question of evolution and its purpose for specifically *human* life, in terms consistent with a Christian understanding of human nature.

This volume offers a unique introduction to his life and ideas. The five essays that comprise BUILDING THE EARTH and the additional essay, THE PSYCHOLOGICAL CONDITIONS OF HUMAN UNIFICATION, display in the simplest way the broad range of his thought, and will stimulate and prepare many readers for his other works.

BUILDING THE EARTH

and

THE PSYCHOLOGICAL CONDITIONS OF HUMAN UNIFICATION

Pierre Teilhard de Chardin

With an introductory essay
on Teilhard de Chardin
by John Kobler

Foreword by Max H. Bégouën
of the *Association of Friends
of Teilhard de Chardin*

PUBLISHED BY AVON

AVON BOOKS
A division of
The Hearst Corporation
959 Eighth Avenue
New York, New York 10019

Library of Congress Catalog Card Number: 65-25559.

First Printing (Discus Edition), April, 1969

Cover photo by Philippe Halsman

DISCUS BOOKS TRADEMARK REG. U.S. PAT. OFF. AND
FOREIGN COUNTRIES, REGISTERED TRADEMARK—
MARCA REGISTRADA, HECHO EN CHICAGO, U.S.A.

Printed in the U.S.A.

This is the first American paperback edition of CONSTRUIRE LA TERRE by Pierre Teilhard de Chardin, originally published by Editions du Seuil (Paris). The translation was made by Noël Lindsay, whose work was officially approved by the *Association of Friends of Teilhard de Chardin.*

The translation of the additional essay in this volume, "The Psychological Conditions of Human Unification," was made by Joseph L. Caulfield.

The Age of Nations is past.
The task before us now,
if we would not perish,
is to build the earth.

Teilhard

Table of Contents

FOREWORD

A luminous scientific mind and a great heart, both of them big enough to encompass the whole world, gave Teilhard de Chardin the vision and the power, as long ago as 1937, to discern the rising tide of destructive forces which threaten our planet. And they led him to call on all mankind to unite in building the earth—in making the world a home for all peoples.

The peoples of the earth, "the natural units of humanity" as he called them, must (he declared) achieve earthly harmony through the very variety of their racial characteristics—characteristics which reciprocally enrich one another. He gave each of them this watchword: "Remain true to yourselves, but move ever upward toward greater consciousness and greater love! At the summit you will find yourselves united with all those who, from every direction, have made the same ascent. *For everything that rises must converge.*"

Just as the various cells and members of the body grow and unite to form a single living being and find their ultimate perfection only by constituting that being, so the constant goal of individual and national development should (in Teilhard's view) be the unity of mankind. Both individuals and nations must achieve this unity, he wrote, if we are ever to have any fulness of life on the earth.

This latter goal is still largely unattained, but there exists in all the countries of the world today a new ferment toward this end, a secret aspiration for what Teilhard perceived at a distance. May these countries be delivered from the fatal temptation of building for themselves alone; the sap which is rising in them is not destined to their own selfish ambitions but to the common achievement of all peoples, of mankind.

"*The Age of Nations is past,*" wrote Teilhard. "*The task before us now, if we would not perish, is to build the earth.*"

May there be an end to those hostile factions among us which stir up the forces of destruction to a frenzy. Let there be manifested instead a spirit of universal cooperation inspired by Teilhard's vision, by a passion to construct a world worthy of man. The value of any vision is not tested by force; it does not need the atom bomb in order to convince; its measure and its meaning are in the positive energies it can wrest from the womb of humanity. So Teilhard de Chardin taught us many years ago, and he affirmed further that above all the moribund ideologies there was one incomparably vast and powerful ideal. To this ideal he had devoted himself with all his heart, and his enthusiasm for it caused us to work with him for its fulfillment.

A social or ethnic group which can find no better answer to the tragic circumstances of life today than to increase its own selfish demands, shows by that very fact its own moral bankruptcy. By contrast love, which is the supreme form of human dedication and its greatest beauty, makes no demands; it simply strives and progresses. It realizes what the conditions of mankind should be and, brushing all obstacles aside, leads us onward to purify, elevate and fulfill the earth.

Despite the crushing burdens which selfish revolutions place on mankind today, the substance of a new world is being born in the very flesh of peoples all over the earth. Following in the steps of Teilhard, it is our task to bring this new world to fruition; to help the world concentrate all energies in the quest for peace; and in every country help prepare men who, at first in the circle around them and then at the head of nations, will preside over the true destiny of mankind.

We must in short be the vanguard of a crusade for human advancement, the call to which is sounded in the following pages by one who, from the summit he so heroically reached, caught a glimpse of the magnificence which might be the earth of man.

Max H. Bégouën

the priest who haunts the catholic world

By John Kobler

WHEN PIERRE TEILHARD DE CHARDIN died in New York City in 1955, the French Jesuit priest and paleontologist was little known outside a circle of fellow priests, scientists and friends. Today he is a symbol of the winds of change that are blowing throughout Christendom. By attempting, in essays, books and lectures, to reconcile and unify science and religion, he has kindled fiercer controversy within his church than any other modern Catholic thinker.

At one extreme of opinion Father Teilhard is acclaimed as "the saint Thomas Aquinas of our age . . . a new Galileo . . . a great scientist and a great servant of God." At the other extreme he is denounced as "the Trojan horse of Catholicism," a man with dangerous theories in which "maximum seduction coincides with maximum aberration." The Holy Office of the Vatican banned Teilhard's works from Catholic bookstores in 1957 (though some ignored the ban) and in 1962 issued a *monitum* [a formal warning] against exposing believers to the perils of Teilhardism. When Pope John convoked the Ecumenical Council, however, he said its task was "to open the windows of the Church . . . bringing it into step with modern times."

The council never openly referred to "the forbidden Jesuit," as one biographer calls Father Teilhard. But the flickerings of his influence glinted beneath the polemics. They did so again during the recent sessions of the council, reconvened by Pope Paul. An Italian expert on the council goes so far as to predict that the outcome will either reflect the Teilhardian spirit or it will accomplish nothing of importance.

Teilhard's influence extends far beyond the domain of Catholic theology. The total sales of his twelve books run to over a million copies. Organizations of dedicated followers labor to increase the boom. In France the Association of the Friends of Teilhard de Chardin, boasting roughly a thousand members, sponsors lectures, symposiums and week-long conventions. Other Teilhardist groups, some of them verging on cultism, flourish in Italy, Germany, England, Belgium and South America. The Teilhard bibliographies list more than twelve hundred titles. The Paris Museum of Natural History opened a wing full of Teilhard documents and memorabilia. The French mint struck a medallion in his honor, bearing his profile and his mystical axiom: "Everything that rises converges." Despite the right-wing hostility to the Jesuit, the Vatican pavilion at the Brussels World's Fair included his portrait in a gallery of the century's greatest men. Even the Communists are trying to exploit Teilhard; one of his books has already been published in Moscow.

Teilhard has become celebrated only after his death because the Society of Jesus forbade him to publish his works during his lifetime. They were saved from oblivion by the devotion of his followers, particularly a woman named Jeanne Mortier, guardian of a cupboard full of his unpublished manuscripts. Barred from teaching or holding ecclesiastical office, Teilhard spent most of his life in exile, often anguished, but always submissive, free of rancor and deeply devout.

Teilhard, who died at the age of seventy three, came of an ancient, wealthy and patrician family. He was a superb physical specimen, tall and sinewy, with the profile of a falcon hewn from rock, but softened by a luminous smile and glowing, gray-blue eyes. He loved people. "The world is round," he used to say, "so that friendship may circle it." A certain sartorial elegance is one of the few little vanities a priest may indulge. Teilhard, however, utterly indifferent to externals, was usually rumpled, and his trousers—for he preferred to wear trousers without the cassock—

seldom met his shoe tops. Though he did not actively proselytize, the power of his conviction and his personal radiance fortified the faith of waverers and moved nonbelievers to join the Church.

Intellectually sophisticated, an aristocrat by birth and breeding, Teilhard yet retained a child-like simplicity and directness, a naïveté, in his social relations which encouraged opportunists to use him. He could not bring himself to condemn any man. Chided for associating with an exceptionally repulsive character, he replied, "No doubt he has other, valuable qualities." A younger brother, Gabriel, an air-force officer at the outset of World War II, wrote to him in angry despair over France's defeat, "The soldiers of 1940 were afraid to die." The Jesuit's answer passed Gabriel's understanding: "They felt they had another and better task to fulfill."

The intelligentsia of Paris, New York and Peking lionized Teilhard, and their salons became forums for the dissemination of his ideas. But he was also accessible to the lowliest student who wanted his guidance. Gay and witty, despite painful inner conflicts, he had a propensity for impish clerical jests which sometimes shocked starchy churchmen. Noting the prim, desiccated old maids who crowded a Paris Jesuit chapel when he celebrated Mass there, he exclaimed, "Lord, Lord, wherever do You seek Your brides!" Of the persecuted seventeenth-century astronomer, Galileo, whose discoveries about the solar system the Catholic Church did not accept for two hundred years, he said, "I keep his bust in my room, because the church owes him at least that much."

Among Teilhard's achievements as a paleontologist were his substantial contributions to the revelations surrounding the famous "Peking man," one of the earliest known hominids or manlike creatures. (Actually, fossil measurements proved "Peking man" to be a woman, and Teilhard named her "Nelly.") It was from his rare combination of scientific and spiritual insights that Teilhard distilled his controversial theory.

For him no unbridgeable gap existed between science and religion. He viewed them as but two threads of the same seamless garment, two aspects of God.

For forty years manuscripts developing that synthesis flowed from Teilhard's pen. They teemed with propositions bound to strike rigid Catholic theologians as heretical. According to his central theme, "Evolution is a general condition to which all theories, all hypotheses all systems must bow and which they must satisfy if they are to be thinkable and true. Evolution is a light illuminating all facts, a curve that all lines must follow."

In his first book published, *The Phenomenon of Man*, which was completed in 1940, Teilhard depicts evolution as the progress of the universe —a progress divinely conceived and therefore irresistible—from elemental matter through the advent of life, animal consciousness and human thought toward God. "Man did not descend from an ape," he was fond of saying. "He ascended." Nine books followed, among them his lyric, passionate spiritual testimony, written in 1927, *The Divine Milieu.*

Widely translated, they have achieved a commercial success in both Europe and the U.S. which astounds the publishing world, for they make formidable demands on the reader. Pope John once complained, "Why did he have to write such difficult things?" At times Teilhard pursues his arguments along paths so labyrinthine that he loses the reader altogether. His brilliant style compounds the difficulties by intermingling the tones of poetry, metaphysics, science, mysticism, philosophy and Scripture. He frequently coins words and gives familiar ones special meanings. To aid bewildered readers, his French publisher brought out a lexicon of his neologisms, such as "*hominization:* the progressive movement of nonreflective animal life towards reflective human life." Yet by the end of 1962, more than seven years ago, *The Phenomenon of Man* had already sold 140,000 copies in France and 50,000 in the United States.

Curiosity partly explains the anomaly, a curiosity stimulated by the long suppression of the manuscripts, the aura of mystery surrounding Teilhard's private life, and the resulting body of legend. Snobbishness is another factor. Teilhard has become fashionable. Dropping the name is a ploy of cocktail-party one-up-manship. Casually displayed on a livingroom table, his works impart highbrow status. But the biggest stimulus to popular success has been the torrent of books and articles about Teilhard.

At New York's Catholic Fordham University, Dr. Louis Marks, then Associate Professor of Biology, taught a seminar on Teilhard. His personal enthusiasm was unqualified. "Teilhardism will become the Church's new philosophical system," he predicted. But in deference to the *monitum*, Dr. Marks exhorted his students to approach the subject with prudence. A waggish sophomore even brought a plaster gargoyle to class. "Here she is," he announced. "Meet Prudence."

Catholic dogma does not require believers to accept Genesis literally. It permits a variety of theories, including evolution, providing they recognize Scripture as divine revelation. Fifteen centuries ago Saint Augustine advised Christians not to consider the Bible a scientific text, and his own commentary on Genesis is often cited to show that evolution can be compatible with orthodoxy. Nevertheless, in practice evolution has long been a risky area for Catholics, because its early proponents were predominantly materialists who dismissed God from the universe. In fact, not until Pope Pius XII's encyclical letter of 1950, *Humani Generis*, did the church explicitly authorize Catholic scholars to explore evolution, and then only as an unproven hypothesis.

In Teilhard's system, however, evolution is no hypothesis. It is the key to the whole meaning of existence. It operates not through blind chance as the scientific materialists argued, but purposefully, an irreversible process planned by God. A twofold principle underlies this process: Nothing can appear that has not been prepared from all eternity, and the universe is always at work perfecting itself.

The starting point of evolution from primordial matter Teilhard called Alpha, and the Goal, the Omega Point. Omega is, in effect, God, but Alpha also contains God. Thus, the universe began in God and will return to Him. "Man," Teilhard wrote, "is not a static center of the world, as he long assumed, but the axis and arrow of evolution, which is something finer." So far the march of evolution has advanced through three major stages—pre-life, life and thought. Hyper-life, for which Teilhard believed man to be now ripe, lies ahead.

> . . . humanity has just entered what is probably the greatest transformation it has ever known. . . . Something is happening in the structure of human consciousness. It is another species of life that is just beginning.

From hyper-life, Teilhard prophesied, with the radiant optimism that colored his vision, humanity individually and collectively will eventually enter into ultimate, perfect union with God at the Omega Point, and so will conclude the epic drama of evolution. Nothing, he felt, could prevent that final consummation.

As the main forces of evolution, Teilhard posited two kinds of energy. The first kind, "tangential" energy, acts upon what he termed the "Outside of Things." Scientists see the growth of the universe as a sequence of combinations: atoms forming molecules, molecules forming cells, cells forming plants and animals. But the physical and chemical forces that bring about these changes manufacture no new energy. According to the laws of thermodynamics, the new organism expends its energy in heat and eventually disintegrates. Physicists reckon that the sun, for example, will consume all its available hydrogen atoms in about fifteen billion years, then cool off and die. "A rocket rising in the wake of time's arrow that bursts only to be extinguished," Teilhard reflected poetically, "an eddy rushing on the bosom of a descending current—such then must be our picture of the world. So says science, and I believe in science, but up to now has science ever troubled to look at the world except from without?"

Teilhard rejected the prospect of the universe thus reduced to a cold, black void, of evolution vanquished. God, he believed, could not have intended such an end for his creation. There must exist some other kind of energy capable of producing higher forms *ad infinitum* and thereby preventing universal decay. Teilhard looked for such an energy on the "Inside of Things," by which he meant consciousness, and he ascribed an inherent consciousness to even the lowest forms of inorganic matter. Operating on the Inside, on consciousness, he concluded, was a "radial" or spiritual energy, separate from but related to tangential energy. Reversing the laws of thermodynamics, he formulated the "Law of Complexity-Consciousness."

According to this law, complexity increases on the Outside until stopped by the loss of tangential energy. But on the Inside, radial energy, which is inexhaustible, drives the organism toward higher levels of both complexity and consciousness. In the evolution of animals, complexity-consciousness reached the level of instinct and awareness, in man, the level of thought, moral judgment, freedom of choice, spirituality.

"Animals merely know," said Teilhard, "but man knows he knows." Since radial energy is a tremendous reservoir, it will go on producing more and more complex forms and so outdistance the rate of atomic disintegration.

Through this interplay of the Outside and the Inside, Teilhard reinterpreted evolution, the universe and God. Geologists describing the successive layers of the earth speak of the barysphere, composed of metals; the lithosphere, of rocks; the hydrosphere, of water. Teilhard invented a new layer, the noösphere (from the Greek *noos:* mind). Thought, he explained, generated the noösphere. "The idea is that of the earth not only becoming covered by myriads of grains of thought but becoming enclosed in a single thinking envelope so as to form, functionally, no more than a single vast grain of thought. . . ."

But the noösphere is not the apex of evolution. Beyond it, Teilhard believed, beckons a further series of syntheses converging toward the Omega Point. The prerequisite to this final ascent is man's social consciousness. Just as aggregates of cells form an individual, so the aggregate of individuals will form a superorganism, a collective, combining the sum total of human consciousness. But how can personality and collectivity combine without damage to either? Teilhard finds the answer in a special property of radial energy—love. And the power that moves the universe through love toward the zenith is Christianity. In the culminating synthesis of evolution a universal consciousness, forever freed from material shackles, will fuse with Omega.

If left solely to the Holy Office, then headed by the aged, archconservative Alfredo Cardinal Ottaviani, the controversial literature would not only have been banned from Catholic bookstores but also no doubt placed on the Catholic Index of Prohibited Books. Many authors have been proscribed for less. But Pope John took a broader view. He showed scant enthusiasm for the Index. "I am here to bless, not to condemn," he once remarked when asked what fate he thought Teilhard's works deserved, and he had no wish to arouse world opinion with another Galileo case. Indeed, though he approved the *monitum*, a formal warning, probably to appease the Holy Office, he later called it "regrettable." It remains to be seen what position Pope Paul will take.

It is what Teilhard omitted from his account of evolution, or what he failed to stress, that dismays the orthodox. Nowhere, they protest, did he clearly acknowledge spontaneous creation, that act in which God created the human soul. Again, if evolution is carrying humanity infallibly to absolute perfection, if the process was preordained from Alpha to Omega, what place remains for Divine Grace, without which no Christian can achieve salvation? And what happens to evolution if a Third World War annihilates mankind? Part of Teilhard's attraction is his spirit of hope in a time of despair. Some religious thinkers, however, do not share his optimism. "I can base my life on the hope of individual salvation, but not on the certainty of universal survival," said the distinguished French Jesuit theologian, Father Jean Daniélou. "Some imbecile may drop the bomb." Teilhard never dealt logically with the possibility that mankind might destroy itself. In his radiant optimism he simply refused to consider such a possibility could occur.

Teilhard's critics also attack him on scientific grounds. To ascribe consciousness to matter, they object, is sheer mysticism, unverifiable by any instrument of observation.

Yet despite Teilhard's deviations from Christian doctrine and scientific logic, both theologians and scientists agree that he filled an urgent need in both their spheres. Scientific materialism is on the wane. So is religious isolationism. The deeper science probes nature the less likely it seems that science can explain everything, that superhuman power plays no part. At the same time progressive clergymen feel the church must readjust its outlook to the discoveries of modern science, if it is to remain a vital influence.

In his introduction to the English translation of *The Phenomenon of Man*, the agnostic biologist, Sir Julian Huxley, wrote, ". . . [Teilhard] has forced theologians to view their ideas in the new perspective of evolution and scientists to see the spiritual implications of their knowledge. He has both clarified and unified our vision of reality." Maurice Cardinal Feltin, Archbishop of Paris, declared, "What is most alluring in his work is the wonderful prospect of a total aggregate perspective of the universe in which matter and spirit, body and soul, nature and the supernatural, science and faith will find their unity in Christ."

In the United States Father Teilhard's influence has grown enormously. His numerous followers formed an organization. For years there was strong opposition to such a group, the main reason being pressure brought by the Apostolic Delegate, Archbishop Egidio Vagnozzi. One of Teilhard's most ardent American supporters, Father Robert T. Francoeur, a young biology teacher of Steubenville, Ohio, was obliged to abandon his efforts to establish a Teilhardist center, and his anthology, *The World of Teilhard de Chardin*, was banned from Catholic seminaries. Abroad, however, Teilhard has even been dragged onto the tumultuous stage of international politics and there made to serve diametrically opposite aims.

Leopold Sédar Senghor, the French-educated Catholic President of Senegal and black Africa's foremost poet, advances the Jesuit's ideas as an antidote to Communism. Owing mainly to Senghor, Teilhardism has created a considerable ripple on the dark continent.

"Considering the failure of liberal capitalism and the selfishness of privileged nations, our greatest temptation was to turn to Marxism," Senghor proclaimed not very long ago. "We soon realized that if Marxism could help us cure our under-development, it could not satisfy our spiritual hunger. Father Teilhard enabled us to transcend the paradox of materialism and spirituality. He led us out of a dead end."

Although Teilhard's writings contain no direct reference to the problems of Africa's blacks, it is easy to understand how deeply some of his general propositions would appeal to them. For example: "No evolutionary future awaits man except in association with other men. . . . The most humanized groups appear always, in the end, as the product not of a segregation, but of a synthesis."

It is less easy to understand what common ground could possibly exist between Teilhardism and Communism. In the latter Teilhard saw "the most ghastly fetters . . . the anthill instead of brotherhood." Yet one of Teilhard's principal supporters in France, Roger Garaudy, a former Communist senator, head of the Center for Marxist Studies in Paris, and regularly journied to Moscow on Party business. By perverting Teilhard's evolutionary theory, and promoting the idea of collective consciousness only so far as it might lead to a superior social world community, Garaudy made the Jesuit acceptable to the Soviets, who issued a Russian translation of *The Phenomenon of Man* with a preface by Garaudy (one of whose own books is titled *God Is Dead*).

According to the Friends of Teilhard's somewhat naïve justification for thus harboring a Communist, wherever the Teilhardism light shines it can produce only good. But the strange relationship has fortified the anti-Teilhard camp. "We always knew it," they say. "Teilhard undermines Catholicism."

Teilhard's sense of spirit pervading matter germinated in his boyhood. The place was Sarcenat, a tiny mountain village in the province of Auvergne, where the family occupied a majestic eighteenth-century French manor house. "I was certainly no more than six or seven," Teilhard recalled near the end of his career, "when I began to feel drawn by matter—or more exactly by something that 'shone' at the heart of matter." The boy secretly hoarded commonplace metallic objects—a plow key, nails, spent cartridge shells—and worshiped them as idols. "I withdrew into the contemplation of my 'God of Iron.' Why iron? Because in my childish experience nothing was harder, tougher, more durable. Stability:

That undoubtedly has been for me the fundamental attribute of Being."

Despair overwhelmed him when he realized iron rusted. To console himself, he searched for more durable idols. The region around Sarcenat abounds in volcanic craters, and he dug up bits of quartz, amethyst and chalcedony. His entire spiritual life, as he looked back on it, semed to him merely a development of that boyhood vision. So did his dedication to paleontology.

The name "Teilhard" is among the oldest in the Auvergne ("de Chardin" was added after a nineteenth-century marriage). Genealogists trace it to a fourteenth-century notary, Pierre Teilhard. In 1538 noble rank was conferred upon one Astorg Teillard, as the name was also spelled. For his heraldic shield Astorg chose an exalted motto: "Fiery their vigor and celestial their origin."

Pierre Teilhard de Chardin's mother, Berthe Adèle de Dompierre d'Hornoy, was a woman so pious that when a priest tried to give her some comfort on the death of one of her children, she told him, "No, why trouble? He is in heaven before us." She had a plaque raised over the main entrance of the manor house, consecrating it to "the Sacred Heart of Jesus." In order to be on hand when her children awoke, she normally attended the earliest Mass at the village church, which was celebrated before dawn, walking the two miles, rain or shine, even during her pregnancies. At home she had her own oratory where she frequently retired with her rosary. To his "dear and sainted mother," Pierre attested, "I owe the best in my soul. . . . It gives me great strength to know that the whole effort of evolution is reducible to the justification and development of a love of God. That is what my mother used to tell me long ago." Ironically, the Teilhard de Chardin genealogy derives its loftiest distinction from her great-great-granduncle, the anti-clericalist, Voltaire. She often prayed for his soul.

On inherited land—the accumulation of generations—Pierre's father, Emmanuel, led the life of a country squire. An erudite man, with a passion for original historical documents, he tirelessly rooted through the provincial archives. His efforts were crowned by the discovery of a letter Joan of Arc had dictated, bearing her full signature—the only specimen known—instead of her customary "X." Emmanuel also had a taste for natural science which he imparted to Pierre. But he never quite accepted the twentieth century. To his dying day he wrote with a quill pen. He did not install electricity or central heating in his house until the Thirties. He looked upon trade and commerce as demeaning pursuits, and when his son Joseph went into the shipping business (the last surviving child, and head of a Paris insurance company), the old gentleman felt the family escutcheon had been stained. As another son, Albéric, had once observed, "We are a family who should be preserved under glass."

Pierre was born on May 1, 1881, the fourth of eleven children. They were all handsome, intelligent and godly, and all but three died young of disease or battle wounds in World War I. Smallpox killed his sister Françoise at the age of twenty-six in Shanghai, where she was the mother superior of a renowned convent. His sister Marguerite-Marie, for whom he had a particular spiritual affinity, contracted tuberculosis of the spine at twenty, and during the seventeen years left to her she was bedridden. Yet by correspondence and bedside conferences she directed the Catholic Association of the Sick. Years after her death Pierre apostrophized her in these words:

"O Marguerite, my sister, while I, dedicated to the positive forces of the universe, was wandering over the continents and the seas, passionately absorbed in watching all the hues of the earth rise, you, motionless, prostrate, you were silently transforming, at the depths of your being, the darkest shadows of the world into light.

"In the eyes of the Creator, tell me, which of us two will have played the better role?"

Like all the boys of the family, Pierre went to a Jesuit school. (All the girls attended an Ursuline convent.) He won top honors in every subject but one—religious doctrine. The fusty method of teaching it repelled him. At eighteen, having passed his baccalaureate, he entered a Jesuit novitiate. He had barely taken his first vows, in 1901, when the French government enacted harsh anticlerical laws, and he migrated with his order. England offered the Jesuits refuge first on her channel island of Jersey, then in Brighton. When not occupied by his curriculum, which consisted chiefly of philosophy and the physical sciences, Teilhard roved the countryside with a geologist's hammer.

A Jesuit's religious preparation is long and rigorous, and he was not ordained until 1911. By then the anti-clericalism at home had subsided, and the Jesuits returned. Father Teilhard was attached to the paleontological laboratory of the Paris Museum of Natural History.

World War I brought a shattering spiritual crisis to Teilhard. He joined a regiment of Moroccan Zouaves as a stretcher-bearer. Under the heaviest barrage he would venture deep into no-man's-land after the wounded as if bullets were air. His valor won him the Military Medal and the knighthood of the Legion of Honor. The Moroccan soldiers believed he was protected by his *baraka*, an Arabic word meaning spiritual stature. A young officer he befriended, Max Bégouën,* marveled at such serenity in the face of death. "If I'm killed," said Teilhard, "I shall have changed my state, that's all."

* Author of the Foreword to this edition.

His evolutionary concept had begun to take shape, and despite the exhaustion of battle, he would spend half the night pacing up and down behind the trenches, thinking. "Except for a few bad hours," he said in his old age, "I never lost my taste for thought."

Neither war nor natural cataclysms could shake his belief in the infallibility of evolution. To Teilhard mankind was imperishable. Evil, suffering, waste he saw as only transient departures from the main thrust forward, necessary departures, "because His perfections cannot run counter to the nature of things, and because a world, assumed to be progressing towards perfection, is of its nature precisely still partially disorganized. A world without a trace or a threat of evil would be a world already consummated. . . . Like an artist making use of a fault or an impurity in the stone he is sculpting or the bronze he is casting so as to produce more exquisite lines or a more beautiful tone, God, without sparing us the partial deaths, nor the final death, which forms an essential part of our lives, transfigures them by integrating them in a better plan. . . ." Again, Teilhard could not accept the idea that mankind might commit suicide.

Shortly after the armistice, Max Bégouën, whom the war had reduced to a spiritual vacuum, met Teilhard at a dinner party in Paris, and they left together. Bégouën recounts:

> It was raining and cold. As I walked beside him, I told him I had lost my faith and why. Very simply, with the kindness and charity that never failed him, he expounded his ideas on creation, the meaning of evolution, and the supreme and active part Christ played in the evolution of the cosmos. From nine to midnight, walking back and forth in the rain, Father Teilhard . . . gave me the answer I had waited for so long. That night I was reborn, tottering like Lazarus as he stepped out of the tomb at God's command: Come forth.

Teilhard was then completing his scientific studies at the Sorbonne. The following year the Catholic Institute of Paris appointed him to its chair of geology. In 1923 his superiors permitted him to join an expedition into the Ordos Desert of Inner Mongolia. He was gone three years. One Easter Sunday, camping near the edge of the desert, he had the original inspiration for a remarkable prayer:

> Since once again, O Lord, in the steppes of Asia, I have no bread, no wine, no altar, I will raise myself above those symbols to the pure majesty of Reality, and I will offer to You, I, Your priest, upon the altar of the entire earth, the labor and the suffering of the world. . . .
>
> "Receive, O Lord, in its totality, the Host which Creation, drawn by Your magnetism,

presents to You at the dawn of a new day. This bread, our effort, is in itself, I know, nothing but an immense disintegration. This wine, our anguish, as yet, alas! is only an evaporating beverage. But in the depths of this inchoate mass You have placed—I am certain, for I feel it—an irresistible and holy desire that moves us all, the impious as well as the faithful, to cry out: 'O Lord, make us one!'

Returning to Paris, he resumed his chair at the Catholic Institute. His tenure was brief. While his novel religio-scientific synthesis, his lyricism and his quips packed the classroom, they disturbed the Society of Jesus. When he wrote an essay suggesting that original sin was not a historical fact but largely a theory to explain the existence of evil, his superiors ordered him for his own sake, before Rome took action, to stop teaching and stick to scientific research, preferably far from France. Under the auspices of the Museum of Natural History, Teilhard obediently sailed back to China.

The society might have thought better of banishing him had it foreseen how his scientific work with Peking Man and other fossil discoveries in China, India and Africa would confirm him in his objectionable theory.

"Where the goat is tethered," he said later, "there must he graze, but in the little freedom allowed me I intend to strike as much fire as I can."

Although many of the Jesuits personally revered Teilhard and felt he would add luster to their history, the Father General in Rome, John Janssens, refused to lift the ban on his writings. "I pray I may never grow bitter," Teilhard said to a Jesuit friend. He never did. But he sometimes wondered whether he had the moral right to accept a life of silence. He answered his own question in a poignant letter to another Jesuit:

> If I rebelled (humanly, it would be so easy and so sweet), I would betray my belief that Our Lord activates all events. Moreover, I would compromise the religious value of my ideas in the eyes of our own brothers, if not others. They would see an estrangement from the church, pride, who knows what. It is essential I show, by my example, that if my ideas are novel, they make me no less faithful. But there are shadows. Which of my two vocations is more sacred—the one I followed in my boyhood, at eighteen, or the one revealed to me in the fullness of my manhood as the true meaning? Oh, my friend, tell me that by obeying I am not being false to my ideals.

In 1939, during a short visit to Paris, Teilhard gave several private lectures. His listeners included Jeanne Mortier, a tiny, graying, birdlike spinster whose home, then as now, was one room she rented in a convent, and who performed various volunteer educational chores for the church. "Father Teilhard's message immediately became vital to my spiritual life," she recalls. Offering to serve him as a secretary at no pay, she persuaded him to entrust her with his manuscripts. Out of her meager pocketbook she met the cost of having copies made by mimeograph, as many as five hundred per manuscript, and she circulated them among people partial to Teilhard's views.

Was this tantamount to defying the church, as Teilhard's enemies charge? He never thought so. By publication he understood books sold in bookstores, not copies of manuscripts privately distributed. At any rate, neither the Father General nor the Holy Office called him to account. A number of the Paris Jesuits actually abetted Mlle. Mortier in her efforts to propagate Teilhardism. After the priest returned to China, she organized discussion groups which eventually led to the Association of the Friends of Teilhard.

World War II caught him in Peking, and he did not see France again for six years. Assisted by another marooned Jesuit and scientist, Father Pierre Leroy, he launched the Geobiological Institute, one of whose ambitious projects it was to investigate the prehistory of the entire Asian continent. The war, however, cut off the subsidies he had been getting from both French and Chinese foundations, the Japanese invasion restricted his movements, and he had to content himself with minor laboratory research. He was often cold, hungry and ragged. But outwardly he retained all his sparkle, *bonhomie* and tolerance. Father Leroy once chaffed him, "If you met the Devil himself, you'd think of something nice to say."

"Yes, why not?" Teilhard agreed.

Of the church dignitaries who judged his writings heretical, he remarked with a sly grin, "They're not ripe yet. Evolution hasn't quite touched them." Only a few intimate companions know what inner torment Teilhard suffered. Several times Leroy found him weeping and close to nervous collapse. But even in his blackest moods he would declare, "God is great. One must obey."

It was in Peking that he finished *The Phenomenon of Man.* He gave the manuscript to an American friend, Mrs. John Wiley, as she left for the United States with her husband, a foreign-service officer, asking her to keep it until she heard from him or, should he die in China, to forward it to a certain American Jesuit. It eventually reached Jeanne Mortier. In her published memoirs, Mrs. Wiley wrote, "Never until I met Father Teilhard did I so deeply feel the truth of the words of Genesis: 'So God created man in His own image, in the image of God created He him.' "

When Teilhard finally got back to France, after the war, he was worn out by physical privation and emotional stress. Soon after, he had a heart attack. He recovered only to face new repressive measures. The Society barred his way to the highest academic post open to him—a professorship at the august College de France. (The Academy of Sciences, however, elected him a member; the government appointed him to an important post with the National Center for Scientific Research, and raised him to higher rank in the Legion of Honor.) He decided to appeal personally to Father General Janssens. "I am going to stroke the tiger's whiskers," he told his friends. He returned from Rome in tears. "They don't want me to write," he said. "They don't want me to think. They want me to disappear."

He entered his last exile in 1951 as a member of the Wenner-Gren Foundation for Anthropological Research, undertaking first a field study of early South African man, then settling at the foundation's New York headquarters. From Cape Town he wrote to Father Janssens:

> Above all I feel that you must resign yourself to taking me as I am, that is, with the congenital quality (or weakness) which ever since my childhood has caused my spiritual life to be completely dominated by a sort of profound 'feeling' for the organic realness of the World. . . .
>
> I now feel more indissolubly bound to the hierarchal Church and to the Christ of the Gos-

pel than ever before in my life. Never has Christ seemed to me more real, more personal or more immense.

How, then, can I believe that there is any evil in the road I am following?

I fully recognize, of course, that Rome may have its own reasons for judging that, in its present form, my concept of Christianity may be premature or incomplete and that at the present moment its wider diffusion may therefore be inopportune.

It is on this point of formal loyalty and obedience that I am particularly anxious to assure you that, in spite of apparent evidence to the contrary, I am resolved to remain a "child of obedience."

Teilhard's manuscripts now filled a huge cupboard in Jeanne Mortier's convent room, and before leaving Paris he named her his legatee, thus empowering her to have them published after his death. For that act he has been sharply criticized. A Jesuit may not make a will. Upon taking his vows he relinquishes all material possessions to the Society. But in vindication of Teilhard his partisans repeat what the late Father Raymond Jouve, administrator of the prestigious Jesuit review, *Études*, told him: The vow of poverty does not cover manuscripts; the author may dispose of them outside the Society without violating any canonical law. "Save your works from oblivion,"

Jouve urged Teilhard. "If we inherit them, they will never see the light of day. Appoint a literary executor."

During his years in New York Teilhard touched many lives and, as he had everywhere, he left a trail of bright and warm memories. One who knew him, the sculptress Malvina Hoffman, an ailing but still beautiful woman at seventy-six, sat sipping Bourbon and water in the studio where Teilhard had posed for a bust that now stands in the Paris Museum of Modern Art. "To be ready for death is the sense of life—he taught me that," she recalled, "and when I lay near death after a coronary, it helped me through." She raised her glass. "Here's to him, wherever he is. God bless him."

Father Robert Gannon, the former rector of New York's St. Ignatius Loyola parish, spoke of Teilhard's humility: "It's customary for a young Jesuit to have a monthly spiritual consultation with his superior. Not the older priests, though. But Pierre, busy as he was, and living in rooms outside the parish, would come to me every month as humbly as the youngest novice."

Teilhard had often prayed God to accord him at his death a special sign of communion. In *The Divine Milieu* he wrote:

> . . . when I feel I am losing hold of myself, absolutely passive in the hands of the great un-

known forces that have shaped me, in those dark moments, grant, O God, that I may understand that it is You who are painfully parting the fibers of my being in order to penetrate the very marrow of my substance, and bear me away with You. . . . O divine Energy, ineluctable and vivifying Power, because, of us two, You are infinitely the stronger, it is to You that the role falls of consuming me in the union which should weld us together. Grant me, therefore, something still more precious than the grace for which all the faithful pray. It is not enough that I should die while communicating. Teach me to communicate while dying.

Twenty eight years later, on a March evening in 1955, during dinner with some compatriots, he voiced the hope that when his hour struck it would be the Day of Resurrection.

Easter fell on April 10 that year. The sky was a limpid blue, the air soft. In the morning, following his private Mass, he attended a pontifical Mass at St. Patrick's Cathedral. Before lunch he strolled through Central Park, revolving in his mind, perhaps, the essay entitled *Le Christique*, which he had recently mailed to Mlle. Mortier. It described Christ as a presence irradiating evolution. In the afternoon Teilhard went with old friends, Mrs. Rhoda de Terra and her daughter, Noel, to the New York City Center. The attraction was that familiar combination, *Cavalleria Rusticana* and *Pagliacci*. Afterward they walked back to Mrs. de Terra's apartment off Fifth Avenue for tea.

Teilhard was exulting over the splendor of that Easter Sunday, the loveliest, he said, he had ever known, when, in midspeech, he pitched to the floor unconscious. As Mrs. de Terra put a pillow under his head, he opened his eyes. "What happened to me? Where am I?"

"You're in my home," she said. "Do you recognize me?"

"Yes. But what happened? I don't remember anything. . . . This time, it's terrible."

Mrs. de Terra sent for a doctor and a priest. Before either arrived, Teilhard's heart had stopped.

Jesuits shun funeral pomp. The service at St. Ignatius Loyola Church was simple to the point of poverty. Ten mourners attended, among them Father Leroy, who happened to be in the country for a scientific congress. He alone accompanied the body to the cemetery of the Jesuit novitiate, seventy-five miles upstate, at Saint Andrews-on-the-Hudson. A cross of white flowers adorned the grave. It came from Malvina Hoffman. The small headstone bore only Teilhard's name and the dates of his birth and death.

When Jeanne Mortier heard the news, her first thought was, "Now there's nobody whom I can ask the great questions." For three days she kept to her room, grieving. Then she unlocked her manuscript-crammed cupboard and took out *The Phenomenon of Man.*

She had already chosen one of France's ablest publishers, Paul Flamand, a Catholic, upon condition that no matter what pressures the church might exert, he would not alter a word. There were strong pressures. Emissaries from the Holy Office threatened them both with the Index. But they both stood firm. "So much the worse," said the iron-willed little woman. "I prefer the Index to depriving the world of such masterpieces."

The Phenomenon of Man came out within eight months of Teilhard's death. The royalties earned by that and other manuscripts to emerge from Mlle. Mortier's cupboard exceed $150,000 to date. As the author's closest living kinsman, Joseph Teilhard de Chardin considered contesting her right to the legacy. When, however, he learned she was not keeping a cent for herself, but devoting it all to the furtherance of his brother's teachings, he waived any claims he might have.

Hostile voices continue to bedevil Mlle. Mortier, but fail to budge her, for she clings to what Teilhard wrote in *Le Christique:*

> "Let truth appear but once to a single soul, and nothing can ever stop it from invading everything and setting everything ablaze."

I

We must save mankind

There is now incontrovertible evidence that mankind has just entered upon the greatest period of change the world has ever known. The ills from which we are suffering have had their seat in the very foundations of human thought. But today something is happening to the whole structure of human consciousness. A fresh kind of life is starting.

In the face of such an upheaval, actually shaken by it, no one can remain indifferent.

Swept along by the tide of affairs, what can we do to see clearly and to act decisively?

No matter what reactions we may have to current events, we ought first to reaffirm a robust faith in the destiny of man. Even if that faith is already there, it must be fortified.

It is too easy to find an excuse for inaction by pleading the decadence of civilization, or even the imminent end of the world.

This defeatism, whether it be innate or acquired or a mere affectation, seems to me the besetting temptation of our time. Defeatism is invariably unhealthy and impotent; can we also prove that it is unjustified? I think so.

For anyone who can read the chart of facts recorded by modern science, it is now clear that mankind is not an accidental phenomenon occurring by chance on one of the smallest stars in the sky. Mankind represents the culmination of the whole movement of matter and life, so far as it is within the range of our experience. Is there any need to emphasize what strength the believer derives from this recognition on the part of science that the work of creation is a grand design of a Personal Being. Man, the finished prototype whose perfection makes everything prior to him seem like a rough sketch, the keystone of the arch toward which the architectonic lines of the entire edifice converge, Man, in these new perspectives understands better his title to the sovereignty of the universe.

Entirely different from the old anthropocentric view, under which man was the static geometric center of the universe, this view that the "human phenomenon" is the supremely characteristic form of the cosmic phenomenon has an incalculable moral significance; it transforms our values, and guarantees the permanency of the work which we are doing, or rather of the work which is being done through our agency.

Today's critical events mark a turning-point as well as a crisis in our understanding of progress. This we can and must believe; we are progressing.

But in what direction are we moving?

And, above all, what exactly is happening in the profound depths of human society? We are progressing; let us suppose this to be true, but why is there still so much disorder around us?

There are three major influences confronting each other and struggling for possession of the earth.

Democracy, Communism, Fascism.* Whence do these three forces derive their strength, and why is the warfare between them so implacable?

In these three conflicting ideologies it is possible to recognize clearly, though still not completely, the three aspirations which are characteristic of a faith in the future; a passion for the future, a passion for the universal and a passion for the individual; all three of them misunderstood, or imperfectly comprehended; these are the three-fold main springs which keep human energies in a state of tension and conflict all around us.

The case of Democracy is clear enough; two faults of perspective, logically linked with each other, have enfeebled and vitiated the democratic vision of the World, one affecting its personal-

* The expression Fascism is used throughout to indicate all forms of authoritarian nationalism.

ism, and the other in consequence affecting its universality. The social aspirations of man cannot attain full originality and full value, except in a society which respects man's personal integrity. Because this has not been understood, democracy rather than freeing man has merely emancipated him. Hence the dispersion, strange as it may seem, of a false liberalism both intellectual and social. For with emancipation each cell of society has thought itself free to be its own center. Hence, also, the disastrous equalitarianism which constitutes a threat to any serious construction of a new earth. Democracy, by giving the people control over progress, seems to satisfy the idea of totality. In fact, it achieves only a counterfeit. True universalism rightly claims to incorporate all initiatives, all values without exclusion all the most obscure potentialities of the person. But it is essentially organic and hierarchic. By confounding individualism and personalism, crowd and totality, by fragmenting and leveling the human mass, democracy has run the risk of jeopardizing our innate hopes for the future of mankind. For that reason it has seen Communism break away from it to the left, and all the forms of Fascism rise against it on the right.

In Communism, faith in a universal vibrant humanity was, at least in the beginning, magnificently exalted. The temptation of Russian neo-Marxism for the elite consists far less in its humanitarian gospel than in its vision of a totalitarian civilization strongly linked with the cosmic powers of matter. The true name of Communism should be "terrenism." Unfortunately, here too, the human ideal was defective or very quickly became deformed. On the one hand, in an excessive reaction against the anarchic liberalism of Democracy, Communism soon arrived at the virtual suppression of the individual, and has turned man into a termite. On the other hand, in its unbalanced admiration of the physical powers of the universe, it has systematically excluded from its hopes the possibility of a spiritual metamorphosis of the universe. The human phenomenon (essentially defined by the development of thought) was thenceforth reduced to the mechanical development of a soulless collectivity. Matter has veiled the spirit. Pseudo-determinism has killed love. The lack of personalism, involving a limitation or even a perversion of the future and undermining in consequence even the possibility of universalism such (rather than any of its economic reverses) are the real dangers of Bolshevism.

There can be no doubt that the Fascist movement was largely out of reaction to the so-called "ideas of the Revolution." And this origin explains the compromising support that it has not ceased to find among the numerous elements interested (for various social or intellectual reasons) in not believing in a human future. But passion is not inspired by stagnation, and there is no lack of ardor in Fascism. It is open to the future. Its ambition is to embrace vast entities within its empire. The sad thing is that the sphere which it contemplates is restricted. Fascism seems deliberately to overlook the vital human element, the unshakeable material basis, which, here and now, have already brought civilization into the international phase. Fascism is obstinately determined to conceive and to build the modern world in the dimensions of a by-gone age. It gives preference to the race over mankind; it wishes to restore a soul to its own people, but it is indifferent to a soulless world. It charts a course into the future in the search for forms of civilization which have vanished forever.

The forces which confront each other all around us are not purely destructive; each of them includes some positive constituents. By virtue of these very constituents, they are unwittingly converging towards a common conception of the future. But in each of them the world is struggling to achieve itself, striving to turn toward the light. This is the crisis of birth, however, not the signs of death. It indicates essential affinities, not eternal opposition.

Once we have distinguished this much inside the currents and in the turmoil of history, we can determine the maneuver which will save us.

How can we unite all the positive values of civilization in a totality which will also respect individual values? How can we attain that higher passionate unity in which we shall find rooted and consummated in a new synthesis the Democratic sense of the rights of the person, the Communist vision of the potentialities contained in matter, and the Fascist ideal of an organized élite?

Fundamentally, in spite of the apparent enthusiasm with which large sections of mankind go along with the political and social currents of the day, the mass of mankind remains dissatisfied. It is impossible to find, either on the right or the left, a truly progressive mind which does not confess to at least a partial disillusionment with all existing movements. A man joins one party or the other, because if he wishes to act he must make a choice. But, having taken his stand, everyone feels to some extent hampered, thwarted, even revolted. Everyone wants something larger, finer, better for mankind.

Scattered throughout the apparently hostile masses which are fighting each other, there are elements everywhere which are only waiting for a shock in order to re-orientate themselves and unite. All that is needed is that the right ray of light should fall upon these men as upon a cloud of particles, that an appeal should be sounded which responds to their internal needs, and across all denominations, across all the conventional barriers which still exist, we shall see the living atoms of the universe seek each other out, find each other and organize themselves. In the old days our fathers set out on the great adventure in the name of justice and the rights of man. To us for whom new sciences have opened space and time with dimensions unsuspected by our fathers there are now new challenges. We can no longer measure our efforts by old achievements, no matter how exalting these were in their own time.

That is why our age is weary of the sectionalism which confines human sympathies in watertight compartments. Such sectionalism drags us into an atmosphere where it is no longer possible to breathe. We must have air. We must unite. No more political fronts, but one great crusade for human advancement.

The Democrat, the Communist and the Fascist must jettison the differences and limitations of their systems and pursue to the full the positive aspirations which inspire their enthusiasm, and then, quite naturally, the new spirit will burst the chauvinist bonds which still imprison it; the three currents will find themselves merging in the conception of a common task; namely to promote the spiritual future of the world.

Only relative unanimity to start with; but real unity, to the extent to which all the world is finally at one in recognizing that the function of man is to build and direct the whole of the earth. Having lived for milleniums in self-contradiction, Mankind has now reached a stage of development from which it can, with all its forces, advance forward.

It will be objected that in order to finally constitute a Crusade of Man, there must be some "antagonist" to oppose. For my part, I do not believe in the supreme effectiveness of the instinct of preservation and fear. It is not the fear of perishing, but the ambition to live which has thrown man into the exploration of nature, the conquest of the atmosphere and the heavens. The loadstone which must magnetize and purify the energies in us, whose growing surplus is presently dissipated in useless wars and perverse refinements, I would place, in the last analysis, in the gradual manifestation of some essential object, whose total wealth, more precious than gold, more seductive than any beauty, would be for man grown adult, the Grail and the Eldorado in which the ancient conquerors believed; something tangible, for the possession of which it would be infinitely good to lay down one's life.

For that reason, if a spiritual Human Front began to come about, it would need, alongside the engineers occupied in organizing the resources of the earth and its lines of communication other "technicians" solely concerned with defining and propagating the concrete goals, ever more lofty, upon which the efforts of human activities should be concentrated. Until now, we have rightly been passionate in seeking to unveil the mysteries concealed in matter infinitely great and infinitesimally small mysteries. But an inquiry of much greater importance to the future will be the study of psychic currents and attractions; a science of spiritual energy. Perhaps, impelled by the necessity to build the unity of the World, we shall end by perceiving that the great object unconsciously pursued by science is nothing else than the discovery of God.

Humanity constantly risks becoming absorbed in the secondary matter of philosophic determinism and other mechanistic views of society. But Christianity, speaking on behalf of man's conscience maintains the primacy of reflective thought—it speaks for man as a free person. This it does in the most effective of all ways, not only by the speculative doctrinal defense of the possibility of a centered, but still universal consciousness, but still more by transmitting and developing through its mysticism the meaning and, in some sense, the direct intuition of this center of total convergence. The least that an unbeliever can admit to-day, if he understands the biological situation of the world, is that the figure of Christ (not only as described in a book, but as realized in the concrete in the Christian consciousness) is so far the most perfect approximation to a final and total object toward which the universal human effort can tend without becoming wearied or deformed.

Note: *Father Teilhard de Chardin did not exclude from Christianity anyone who expressly or implicitly believes in* Love. *He knew that the hour is not the same for every man to realize the essential love, cause and purpose of the universe.*

II

The Spirit of Earth

The phrase "Sense of Earth" should be understood to mean the passionate concern of our common destiny which draws the thinking part of life ever further onward. In principle there is no feeling which has a firmer foundation in nature, or greater power. But in fact there is also no feeling which awakens so belatedly, since it can become explicit only when our consciousness has expanded beyond the broadening, but still far too restricted, circles of family, country and race, and has finally discovered that the only truly natural and real human Unity is the Spirit of Earth.

Stimulated by consecutive discoveries which in the space of a hundred years have successively revealed to our generation several important things—first the profundities and significance of time, then the limitless spiritual resources of Matter, and lastly the power of living beings acting in association—it seems that our psyche is in the process of changing. A conquering passion which will sweep away or transform what has hitherto been the immaturity of the earth has begun to show itself. And its salutary action comes just at the right moment to control, awaken, or order the emancipated forces of love, the dormant forces of human unity, and the hesitant forces of research.

a) Love.

Love is the most universal, formidable and mysterious of cosmic energies.

From the point of view of spiritual Evolution, it seems that we might be able to give a name and a value to this strange energy of love. Could it not be, in essence, the attraction which is exercised upon each conscious element by the center of the universe? The call toward the great union, whose attainment is the only real business in nature . . . ? In this hypothesis (which conforms with the findings of psychoanalysis) love is seen as a primitive and universal psychic energy which gives significance to everything around us.

Thus, through woman the universe is really advancing toward man.

If man fails to recognize the true nature and the true object of his love, the disorder which follows is profound and irremediable. Stubbornly trying to gratify a passion which opens on the Infinite with something that is simply inadequate, man desperately tries to make up for the fundamental disequilibrium brought about within him by a restless search for pleasures, especially those of a material character. This is vanity and, in the eyes of anyone who even partly perceives the inestimable value of the "spiritual quantum" of mankind, a frightening waste.

Look quite coldly, as a biologist or an engineer, at the reddening sky over a great city at night. There, and indeed everywhere else, the Earth is continuously dissipating in pure loss its most miraculous power. The earth is burning uselessly. Idly. Wastefully. How much energy do you think is lost to the Spirit of Earth in one night?

Man must instead perceive the universal reality which shines spiritually through the flesh. He will then discover what has so far frustrated and perverted his power to love. Woman is put before him as the attraction and the symbol of the world. He can unite with her only by enlarging himself in turn to the scale of the world. And because the world is always larger, and always unfinished and always in advance of us, to achieve his love Man thus finds himself embarked on a limitless conquest of the Universe. In this sense, Man can reach woman only through the consummation of the universal union.

Love is a sacred reserve of energy, and the very blood stream of spiritual evolution; that is the first discovery we can make from the Sense of Earth.

b) Human Unity.

In singular opposition to the irresistible attraction manifested in Love is the instinctive repulsion which as a general rule drives human beings like molecules, away from each other. This repulsion can in fact result only from the timidity or cowardice of an individual in face of an effort of expansion which would ensure his liberation.

What an increase there is in his powers when, in research or in battle, Man catches the breath of affection or comradeship; what fulfillment when, in the instant of danger or enthusiasm, he finds in a flash that he has glimpsed the wonders of a kindred spirit. These faint glimmerings should help us realize what a formidable power and joy and capacity for action still slumber in the human spirit. Without any doubt men today suffer and vegetate in isolation; they need a superior impulse to intervene and force them to pass beyond the level at which they are immobilized, leading them to discover their profound affinities. The Sense of Earth is the irresistible pressure which will come at the right moment to unite them in a common passion.

The love of interaction (far more important than even attraction) governs different elements as they draw together to sustain union. Who can tell the plenitude of the yet almost unknown quality, the immense fulfillment of fraternal friendships, which, in the Noösphere, will accompany victory over our internal divisions; that is to say our recognition that human unity can be advanced? can even be achieved?

c) Research.

The Spirit of Earth comes to explain to men the reason for their superfluity of love, and the way in which it might be put to use. At the same time, it reveals itself as the force which is destined to get under way and organize the overwhelming mass of human production and discovery.

Is the world condemned to perish in growing, automatically stifled by the excess of its own weight?

By no means; but it is in the process of gathering the elements of a new and better body. The whole question, in this crisis of birth, is the rapid emergence of the soul which by its appearance will organize, lighten and vitalize this mass of stagnant and confused material. But this soul can only be a "conspiracy" of individuals who associate themselves to raise to a new stage the edifice of life. The resources we enjoy today, the powers and secrets of science we have discovered, cannot be absorbed by the narrow system of individual and national divisions which have so far served the leaders of the world. The age of nations is past. The task before us now, if we would not perish, is to shake off our ancient prejudices, and to build the earth.

The more I look at the world as a scientist the

less I see any other possible biological result apart from its active and conscious unity. Life can progress on our planet in the future (and nothing will prevent it from progressing, not even its own internal servitudes) by throwing down the barriers which still wall off human activity, and by giving itself up without hesitation to faith in the future.

We must put in the forefront of our concrete preoccupations the systematic arrangement and exploration of our universe, understood as the true country of mankind. Then material energy will circulate, and (more important still) spiritual energy, now corrupted by the petty jealousies of modern society, will find its natural outlet in the attack launched against the mysteries of the world. The time has come to realize that research is the highest human function, embracing the spirit of war and bright with the splendor of religion. To keep up a constant pressure on the surface of the real, is not that the supreme gesture of faith in Being, and therefore the highest form of adoration? All that is ours, if we understand how to avoid stifling within us the Spirit of Earth.

Whoever wishes to be part of this spirit must die and be born again, for others and for himself. In order to reach this higher plane of humanity he must bring about a complete transformation in his whole sense of values and his whole action.

Yet a little while and the Spirit of Earth will emerge with its specific individuality and its own character and physiognomy. And then, on the surface of the Noösphere, gradually sublimated in thought and passion, ever striving to solve more lofty problems, to possess greater objects, our tension towards being will be at its maximum.

What will happen at this critical stage in the maturation of terrestrial Life? Are we going to be able at that moment to unite with other centers of cosmic life, to continue the labor of universal synthesis on a higher scale? More probably, something else will happen, something which can be glimpsed only when the influence of God is brought into the reckoning.

It would be nursing a great illusion if the man of our times were to think that, having attained a fuller understanding of himself and of the world, he had no further need of religion. There has been a multiplication of systems in which the existence of religion has been interpreted as a psychological phenomenon associated with the childhood of mankind. At its maximum when civilization is beginning, it should gradually fade away, giving place to more positive constructions, from which God (particularly a personal and transcendent God) would be excluded. In reality, for those who can see, the great conflict from which we will have escaped will only consolidate in the world the necessity of faith. Having reached a higher degree of self-mastery, the Spirit of Earth will experience an increasingly vital need to adore; out of universal evolution God emerges in our consciousness as greater and more necessary than ever.

The only possible Motive Power of a life which has reached the stage of Reflection is an Absolute, or in other words a Divine, Term. Religion has sometimes been understood as a mere antidote to our evils, an "opiate." Its true purpose is to sustain and spur on the progress of life. It is the profound need of an Absolute, sought from the start through every progressive form of religion. Once this starting point is realized, it becomes evident that the "religious function" born of hominization and linked thereto is bound to grow continuously with man himself. The more man is man, the more he will feel the need to devote himself to something which is greater than he is. Is it not that which we can ascertain around us? At what moment in the Noösphere has there been a more urgent need to find a faith, a hope to give meaning and soul to the immense organism we are building?

By the capital event of hominization the most "advanced" part of the cosmos found itself personalized. This simple change in a variable introduced for the future a two-fold condition of existence which cannot be escaped.

Since everything in the universe, starting from Man, takes place in the personalized being, the ultimate Term of the universal Convergence must also possess (in a supreme degree) the quality of a Person. To super-animate, without destroying, a universe made up of personal elements, he must himself be a special Center. Thus there reappears, not as a matter of emotion or instinct, but closely linked with contemporary ideas on evolution, the traditional conception of a God exerting an intellectual influence upon immortal beings, distinct from himself.

The current which raises matter should be conceived less as a simple internal impulse than as a tide. The multiple rises, attracted and incorporated by the "Already One."

In the first phase—before Man— the attraction was vitally, but blindly, felt by the world. Since Man, it is awakened (at least partially), in reflective liberty which sustains religion. Religion is not an option or a strictly individual intuition, but represents the long unfolding, the collective experience of all mankind, of the existence of God—God reflecting himself personally on the organized sum of thinking beings, to guarantee a sure result of creation, and to lay down exact laws for man's hesitant activities.

III

human energy

Human Energy presents itself to our view as the term of a vast process in which the whole mass of the universe is involved.

In us the evolution of the world towards the spirit becomes conscious. From that moment, our perfection, our interest, our salvation as elements of creation can only be to press on with this evolution with all our strength. We cannot yet understand exactly where it will lead us, but it would be absurd for us to doubt that it will lead us towards some end of supreme value.

From this there finally emerges in our twentieth century human consciousness, for the first time since the awakening of life on earth, the fundamental problem of Action. No longer, as in the past, for our small selves, for our small family, our small country; but for the salvation and the success of the universe, how must we, modern men, organize around us for the best the maintenance, distribution and progress of human energy?

The first object which should attract the attention of the technician of human energy is to ensure to the human nuclei taken in isolation, their maximum of consistency and efficiency as elements. To perfect individuals so as to confer upon the whole the maximum of power, that is the obvious line to follow for the final success of the operation.

The organization of the human energy of the element, whatever its general methods may be, must culminate in forming at the heart of each element, the greatest possible amount of personality.

But today, while the mass formation of human society is taking place under our eyes and in our consciousness, Man, assuming him to be henceforward fixed in his individual nature, can see a new and boundless field of evolution opened up before him; the field of collective creations, associations, representations and emotions.

How can we lay down any limits to the effects of expansion, penetration and spiritual fusion which would flow from the coherent ordering of our human multitude? This will be a capital phase of history, when all the transformed power of fleets and armies will come in to reinforce that other power which the machine age has lulled somewhat into idleness, and an irresistible tide of liberated energies will mount towards the most progressive circles of the Noösphere. A substantial part of this tide of available energy will immediately be absorbed in the expansion of man in matter. But another part, and that the most precious, will inevitably flow back to the levels of spiritualized energy. Spiritualized Energy is the flower of Cosmic Energy. To dominate and canalize the powers of the air and the sea is all very well. But what is this triumph, compared with the world-wide mastery of human thought and love? In truth, no more magnificent opportunity than this has ever been presented to the hopes and efforts of the earth.

We are very ready to boast of living in a century of enlightenment and science. And yet the truth is quite the reverse; we are still lingering among rudimentary and infantile forms of intellectual conquest. What proportion of activity in the world today, in money, manpower and effort, is devoted to exploring and conquering the still unknown areas of the world?

At present most men still merely understand strength, the key and symbol of violence in its most primitive and savage form of war.

But let the time come, as come it will, when the masses will realize that the true human successes are those which triumph over the mysteries of matter and of life. At that moment a decisive hour will sound for mankind, when the spirit of discovery absorbs all the momentum contained in the spirit of war. It represents in consequence that part of human strength which there is the greatest interest in organizing. What are the main directions in which we can imagine it tending? And in which we can help it to develop, starting in the heart of our individual natures? No doubt in the direction of a decisive flourishing of some of our old powers, accompanied by the acquisition of some additional faculties, and some extended consciousness. Love, as well as thought, is always in full growth in the Noösphere.

The excess of its expanding energy over the daily diminishing needs of human propagation is daily becoming more evident. This means that love is tending, in its fully hominized form, to fulfill a much larger function than the mere call to reproduction. Between Man and Woman, a specific and reciprocal power of sensitization and spiritual fertilization seems in truth to be still slumbering, demanding to be released in an irresistible upsurge toward everything which is truth and beauty. Beyond a certain degree of sublimation, by the unlimited possibilities of intuition and inter-relation which it brings, spiritualized love penetrates into the unknown.

In every field we will begin to live constantly in the presence and with the thought of the whole. There is nothing more significant, from the point of view of human energy, than the spontaneous appearance, and, ultimately, the systematic cultivation of a "cosmic sense" of this kind. Through such a sense, Men cease to be self-contained individuals, and join in a common cause. In them, thenceforth, the spiritual energy of the element is finally ready to integrate itself in the total energy of the Noösphere. But we must not fail to bring out an important point; the perfection and usefulness of each nucleus of human energy in relation to the whole depend in the last resort upon whatever is unique and incommunicable in each of them. The great point to which the technician of the Spirit should direct his attention in dealing with human beings is to leave them the possibility of discovering themselves, in the transformation which he is seeking to bring about in them, and the freedom to differentiate themselves ever more and more.

The first lineaments of a common consciousness contain in themselves a vital need to make themselves clear and to prolong themselves internally. Intellectually, the progress of science is proceeding to construct a synthesis of the laws of Matter and Life, which, fundamentally, is nothing else but a collective act of perception; the world seen in the same coherent perspective by the whole of mankind. Socially, the fusion and intermingling of races are leading directly to the establishment of an equally common form, not merely of language, but of morality and ideals.

The organization of human energy, taken in its entirety, directs itself and impels us towards the ultimate formation, above each personal element, of a common human soul.

The conjunction of activities out of which there will come a collective human soul, supposes as its principle, a common aspiration, actuated by a common hope. To set in motion and sustain such human energy, there must be at the origin an attraction exercised by a desired object.

Since there is neither fusion nor dissolution of individual persons, the Center which they aspire to rejoin, must necessarily be distinct from them, that is, it must have its own personality, its autonomous reality.

For its maintenance and operation the Noösphere physically requires the existence in the universe of a real pole of psychic convergence; a Center different from all other centers, which it "super-centers" by assimilating them; a Person distinct from all other persons, whom it fulfills by uniting them to itself. The world would not function, if there were not, somewhere outside time and space, a cosmic point of total synthesis.

We have just recognized it: by hominization the universe has reached a higher level, where its physico-moral powers gradually assume the form of a fundamental affinity which links individuals to each other and to their transcendent Center. In us and around us the elements of the world go on unceasingly personalizing themselves more and more, by acceding to a Term of unification; itself personal, so much so, that from this Term of ultimate confluence there radiates and to this Term in the last resort there flows back all the essential Energy of the World—that energy which, having generally agitated the cosmic mass, emerges from it to form the Noösphere.

What name must be given to such an influence? One only—Love; Love, the supreme form and the totalizing principle of human energy.

Picture a man who has become conscious of his personal relations with a supreme Person with whom he is led to merge by the whole interplay of cosmic activity. In such a man, and starting from him, a process of unification is launched, marked by the following stages:

–the totalization of every operation in relation to the individual;
–the totalization of the individual in relation to himself;
–and lastly, the totalization of the individual in the collective Man.

All these so-called "Impossibilities" come about under the influence of Love.

Omega, He towards whom all converges, is concurrently He from whom all radiates. Impossible to place him as a focus at the summit of the universe, without at the same time diffusing his presence in the intimate heart of the smallest movement of evolution. What does that mean except that, for anyone who has seen it, everything, however humble, provided it is placed in the line of progress, warms, enlightens and animates itself, and in consequence becomes the subject of total adhesion.

The fact that under the animating influence of Omega every one of our individual actions may become total is in itself a marvellous use of human energy.

But it transpires that, the first transfiguration of our activities just barely launched, they tend to prolong themselves in another even more profound metamorphosis. By the very fact that they become total, each one individually, our actions logically find themselves induced to totalize themselves, taken altogether in a single act.

Here is a veritable synthesis which the love of Omega brings about on the combined cluster of our faculties:

In the superficial course of our existences, there is a difference between seeing and thinking, understanding and loving, giving and receiving, growing and shrinking, living and dying. But what will happen to all these oppositions when their diversity is revealed in Omega as the infinitely varied operation of the same universal contact? Without disappearing in the world to the least degree they will tend to combine in a common resultant, where their plurality, still recognizable, will flourish in ineffable richness. Why should this astonish us? Are we not familiar in a less intense degree with a perfectly parallel phenomenon in our own experience? When a man loves a woman nobly, the result of this overmastering passion, which exalts the being above itself, is that the life of that man, his power to create and to feel, his whole universe, become specifically contained as well as sublimated in his love of that woman. And yet, woman, however necessary to man, in order to reflect, reveal, communicate and "personalize" the world to him, is still not the center of the world!

If, therefore, the love of one being for another shows itself powerful enough to fuse (without confusing) into a single impression the multitude of our perceptions and our emotions, what vibration would not be drawn by our beings from their encounter with Omega?

When, by the progress in our hearts of this love of the whole, we come to feel, extending above the diversity of our efforts and our desires, the exuberant simplicity of an urge in which are mixed and exalted, without loss, the innumerable gradations of passion and action, then in the heart of the mass formed by human energy, we shall each be approaching the plenitude of our effectiveness and our personality.

To totalize without de-personalizing; to save at the same time the whole and the parts. Everyone agrees on this two-fold aim. But how do existing social groups grade the values which in theory they are agreed they want to preserve? By regarding the person as secondary and transitory, and in placing at the head of their program the primacy of pure totality. In all the systems of human organization which confront each other before our eyes, the underlying assumption is that the final state towards which the Noösphere is tending is a body without an individualized soul, an organism without a face, a diffused humanity, an impersonal.

But this starting-point, once admitted, vitiates the whole subsequent course of the operation to the extent of making it impracticable. How, if the universe finally tends to become a thing can it still find place for a Person? If the summit of human evolution is regarded as impersonal in character, the elements which reach it will inevitably, in spite of all efforts to the contrary, see their personality shrinking under its influence. And that is exactly what is happening. Those who work for material progress or racial causes alone strive in vain to achieve freedom; they are fated to be swamped by the determinisms they are constructing. Their very method of thought mechanizes them. And from that moment there is nothing left to control the operations of human energy but brute force—the force which, quite logically, some people to-day would again like to make us worship.

It is not brute force we need, but love, and therefore, as a start, the recognition of a Transcendent which makes universal love possible.

What will happen on the day when, in place of the impersonal Humanity put forward by modern social doctrines as the goal of human effort, we recognize the presence of a conscious Center of total convergence? At that time, the individuals caught up in the irresistible current of human totalization will feel themselves strengthened by the very movement which is bringing them closer together. The more they are grouped under a Personal, the more personal they will themselves become. And that effortlessly, by virtue of the properties of love.

Picture an earth where all men are clearly and primarily decided on advancing together to a passionately desired Being, in whom each recognizes in what was most incommunicable in his neighbor a living participation. In such a world coercion would become unnecessary for the purpose of retaining individuals in the most favorable order for action, of orienting them in the full play of free will towards the best combinations, making them accept the restrictions and sacrifices imposed by a certain human selection and determining them in the end not to squander their capacity for love, but to sublimate it jealously for the purpose of ultimate union.

We have reached a cross-roads in human evolution where the only road which leads forward is towards a common passion.

To continue to place our hopes in a social order achieved by external violence would simply amount to our giving up all hope of carrying the Spirit of Earth to its limits.

But human energy, like the universe itself, the expression of an irresistible and infallible movement, could not be prevented by any obstacle from attaining freely the natural term of its evolution.

Therefore, in spite of all the apparent improbabilities, we are inevitably approaching a new age in which the world will cast off its chains, to give itself up at last to the power of its internal affinities.

We must believe without reservation in the possibility and the necessary consequences of universal love.

The theory and practice of total love have never ceased, since Christ, to become more precise, to transmit and propagate themselves; so that with two thousand years of mystic experience behind us, the contact which we can make with the personal focus of the universe has gained just as much explicit richness as the contact we can make, after two thousand years of science, with the natural spheres of the world. Regarded as a "phylum" of love, Christianity is so living that, at this very moment, we can see it undergoing an extraordinary mutation by elevating itself to a firmer consciousness of its universal value.

Is there not now under way one further metamorphosis, the ultimate one, the passage of the circles to their common Center, the realization of God at the heart of the Noösphere, the apparition of the "Theosphere"?

IV

thoughts on progress

It has become fashionable to-day to mock or to treat with suspicion, anything which looks like faith in the future.

If we are not careful this skepticism will be fatal, for its direct result is to destroy both the love of living and the momentum of mankind.

Firmly based on the general history of the world, as revealed to us by palaeontology, over a period of 300 million years we can make these two assertions, without losing our foothold in dreams:

a) First and foremost, mankind still shows signs of a reserve, a formidable potential of concentration, that is, of progress. Think of the immensity of the powers, ideas and persons not yet discovered or harnessed or born or synthesized. In terms of "energy" and biology, the human race is still very young and very fresh.

b) The earth is still far from having completed its sidereal evolution. True, we can imagine all sorts of catastrophes which might intervene to cut short this great development. But for 300 million years now, Life has been going on paradoxically in the midst of improbability. Does that not indicate that it is marching forward, sustained by some complicity in the motive forces of the Universe?

The real difficulty which faces man is not the certainty that he is the seat of constant progress; it is rather the conception of how this progress can go on for a long time yet at its present rate, without life exploding of itself or blowing up the earth on which it was born. Our modern world was created in less than ten thousand years, and in the last two hundred years it has changed faster than in all the previous milleniums.

The March Forward, Progress, if it is to continue, will not happen by itself. Evolution, by the very mechanism of its syntheses, is constantly acquiring greater freedom.

In practice, what steps must we take in relation to this forward march?

I see two, which can be summarized in five words: a great hope, in common.

a) First, a great hope. This must be born spontaneously in every generous soul in face of the anticipated work, and it also represents the essential impetus without which nothing will be done. A passionate love of growth, of being, that is what we need. Down with the cowards and the skeptics, the pessimists and the unhappy, the weary and the stagnant.

b) In common. On this point also the history of Life is decisive. There is only one way which leads upwards; the one which, through greater organization, leads to greater synthesis and unity. Here again, then, down with the pure individualists, the egoists, who expect to grow by excluding or diminishing their brothers—individually, nationally or racially. Life is moving towards unification. Our hope will only be operative if it is expressed in greater cohesion and human solidarity.

The future of the earth is in our hands. How shall we decide?

A common science merely brings the geometric point of different intelligences nearer together. A common interest, however passionate, merely brings beings into indirect touch, through an impersonal which destroys personality.

It is not our heads or our bodies which we must bring together, but our hearts.

The generating principle of our unification is not finally to be found in the single contemplation of the same truth or in the single desire awakened by something, but in the single attraction exercised by the same Someone.

V

On the Possible Basis of a Common Credo

Once the reality of a Noögenesis is admitted (the concentration and collective march forward of human thought) the believer in the world finds himself obliged to give a growing place in his thoughts on the future to the values of personality and transcendence. Of personality, since a universe on the road of psychic concentration is identically a universe which is becoming personalized. And of transcendence, because a last pole of "cosmic" personalization, if it is to be supremely consistent and unifying, can hardly be conceived except as emerging from elements which it super-personalizes by uniting them.

Still in the same perspective, assuming it is admitted that there is a cosmic genesis of the spirit, the believer in heaven realizes that the mystic transformation of which he dreams presupposes and confirms all the tangible realities and laborious conditions of human progress. To be super-spiritualized in God, must not mankind first be born and grow in conformity with the whole system of what we call evolution?

The sense of earth opening and flowering upwards in the sense of God, and the sense of God rooted and nourished from below in the sense of earth. The transcendent personal God and the universe in evolution, no longer forming two antagonistic poles of attraction, but entering into a hierarchic conjunction to uplift the human mass in a single tide. Such is the notable transformation which the idea of the spiritual evolution of the universe implies in theory and which is beginning to come about in practice in a growing number of minds, free-thinkers as well as believers. The very transformation we are seeking.

The new spirit for a new world. To unify the vital human forces, so lamentably disunited at this moment, the direct and effective way would simply be to sound the alarm and to form a block of all those who either on the right or the left, believe that the great affair for modern mankind is to break its way out by forcing some threshold of greater consciousness. Whether Christians or not, the men who are animated by this conviction form a homogeneous category. Although in the march of mankind they take their stations on opposing wings, they can advance hand in hand, because their attitudes, far from being exclusive, virtually prolong each other, and ask only to be completed. What are they waiting for, in order to set up the common front of all those who believe that the universe is moving forward, and that it is our task to make it move forward? Would not this be the solid nucleus around which to-morrow's unanimity must develop?

In spite of the wave of skepticism which seems to have swept away the hopes (over-simplified and over-materialist) upon which the nineteenth century lived, faith in the future is not dead in our hearts. Better still, it is this hope, deepened and purified, which seems bound to save us. It is not only that the idea of our consciousness of a possible awakening to a super-consciousness daily becomes better based scientifically on experience and more necessary psychologically to keep alive in man the zest for action; in addition, this very idea pushed to its logical conclusion, seems the only one capable of making mankind ready for the great event which we are awaiting; the discovery of a synthetic act of adoration in which are allied and mutually exalted the passionate desire to conquer the world, and the passionate desire to unite ourselves with God; the vital act, specifically new, corresponding to a new age of the earth.

the psychological conditions of human unification

The Psychological Conditions of Human Unification was not originally published as part of BUILDING THE EARTH in the edition published by Dimension Books in 1965. Its first appearance in the U.S. was in Cross Currents Magazine in the Fall of 1952 and is published in this edition by special permission.

IF there is any issue gradually encroaching upon our individual cares, making them a little more intricate every day, surely it is the problem of human unification. All around us, like a flood, the economic, political and psychic totalization of the world never stops invading, and even submerging, the most humble lives.

But what causes, and exactly what is the meaning of this strange and alarming phenomenon?

For a long time, it was still possible for us to believe that the increasing aggregation of Mankind was nothing more than a superficial arrangement of the human units in the search for a more comfortable life.

But today, as a result of a better survey of Time and Space, another idea is about to dawn in our mind. Namely, we begin to realize that, under the veil of human socialization, there may be the same basic and universal force operating which, since the dawn of the world, has constantly striven towards an evergrowing organization of Matter. We must no longer think of this force as a mere spatial motion of the Earth (Galileo), but as the tightening, beyond ourselves and above our heads, of a sort of cosmic vortex, which, after generating each one of us individually, pushes further, through the building of collective units, on its steady course towards a continuous and simultaneous increase of complexity and consciousness.

This being admitted, three important observations have to be made in regard to our historical and biological position as men of the 20th century:

a) First of all, if it is true that the movement of social totalization which is sweeping us along expresses a drift of cosmic magnitude, then we may be confident that it points the safest (and probably the only) way in which we can engage ourselves if we wish not only to survive, but to live abundantly (*supervive*). For is it not by following the main flow of the moving World that we can most surely hope to reach the type of plenitude whose expectation is the motivating force of Life?

b) Next, and because it is the result of a definitely planetary cause (namely, the growing compression of expanding Mankind over the closed surface of the Earth), the unifying process in which we are caught is to some extent, not only healing, but *irresistible.*

c) And yet, however forced upon us is the technicoinvolution of the human world on itself, it remains theoretically possible that, following a defective (and destructive) use of our liberty, we escape the transformation. For, in order to reach Oneness, Man cannot merely accept this process, but must actively cooperate with the cosmic forces which are striving towards unification: a condition which presupposes essentially that he finds *in himself* a strong incentive for unanimization. Any food requires an oven at a right temperature. Similarly, the whole pressure of the Universe will not succeed in integrating the human dust into a single body, unless Man increases accordingly his internal fervor for unification.

Hence, we may say that the bio-economic crisis of Humanity, at the present moment, if reduced to its "crux," comes to this single point:

namely, how to maintain in every man a strong interest in the future of man.

Everybody, today, is concerned with the problem of the world's resources of thermal energy and food. But why is it that nobody seems to be aware of the fact that even with heaps of wheat, mountains of uranium and coal, and oceans of oil, Mankind will starve and decay unless it guards and feeds the source of its vital passion for more power and more vision? Forced from outside to become one, Man will not yield, I repeat, unless he believes passionately in the future of his evolution.

It is with the purpose of solving this urgent and critical problem of Energy that I suggest that we examine:

a) what the structure of the World around us must be,

b) and what must be our soul in our deepest recesses in order that both of them (like two "fiancés") may meet and be caught in the field of a mutual and always increasing attraction.

In other words, let us look:

a) first for the objective,

b) and then for the subjective conditions necessary for the preservation and the growth in Humanity of the psychical ardor which is physically indispensable for the completion of its biological development.

1.—*OBJECTIVE CONDITIONS*

Using a somewhat figurative language, one may say that two main structural characteristics are necessary for the World to fulfill the most basic requests of human nature. First, it has to be *open;* and, second, it has to possess a *center of convergency,* at the ultimate end of its development.

Exactly what do these two expressions mean?

a) *The necessity of an open World.*

Imagine a group of miners cut off by a cave-in, and trying to regain the surface by an escape exit. We know that these men will not seriously fight their way towards the surface unless they have some indication (from a gleam of light, from a draft coming from above) that the ascent is not cut off higher up. Otherwise, they will just sit down and wait, for help—or death.

And similarly, where should Man find the courage to continue the fearful task of advancing the self-unification of Humanity, if this fine effort were to result in nothing but his running against an insurmountable wall?

Because it is of a "reflective" nature, human activity simply could not survive the definite prospect of a *total* disintegration.

Unquestionably therefore, there must be something fallacious in the widely accepted opinion, based on astronomical and biological evidence, that the future of our Species is entirely limited by the physico-chemical evolution of the Earth.

No—decidedly, no. In spite of too many appearances, the World, in order to keep moving, cannot be entirely closed in the future: otherwise Life (Life, I mean, understood in its highest, human form) would stop.

But, above our heads, it has to be in some way open: not only marginally, for a narrow escape—but centrally, for some kind of triumphant achievement.

b) *The necessity of a centered (that is to say of a personalizing) World.*

If a molecule could feel and speak, it would refuse, would it not, to enter into a structure which did not correspond to its particular pattern: such an incorporation would "kill" it.—Similarly Man, because psychologically he is highly centered on himself, will stubbornly resist any process of aggregation unless this process indicates it can respect and increase, in each human particle, the power it possesses to unify, in an infinitesimal but incommunicable way, the World around itself.

However compressed upon itself by planetary constriction, Mankind will revolt against the progress of Socialization so long as this does not present itself as a force, I do not say of egotistic individualization, but of broader personalization.

And this particular effect cannot be obtained unless, as a result of some natural movement of self-convergency, (that is, of mutual attraction), the evolving Universe has the intrinsic requirement of "unanimizing" within a sort of universal "sympathy" the innumerable elements it forces together at the depth of itself.

If we are given a World endowed with this two-fold requirement: not only of having an "upper exit" but also of personalizing whatever succeeds in reaching this ultimate point of emergence—we can then *accept* it.

But how can we "love" it?

Here is revealed the second and psychological (or even the psychoanalytical) aspect of the problem.

2.—*SUBJECTIVE CONDITIONS.*

In order to appreciate a color, a scent, we must have good eyes and a good nose. Exactly in the same way, it is essential that we wake up a certain number of aspirations still half-unconscious in ourselves, if we wish to experience at its full the passion for the ultra-humanization towards which we are impelled by the very drift of the Universe.

At this point, let us again make a comparison. In every human being, in becoming "adult," there emerges what we call the sexual sense. At first indeterminate, and even misunderstood by its subject, the inclination once born grows steadily until it becomes one of the dominating psychological forces of the full-grown individual.

Well, judging from certain symptoms, does it not seem that Mankind, taken as a whole, is actually in the process of undergoing, in its own way, a kind of "crisis of puberty"?

Most certainly, in the Man of today (because he is more aware than a century ago of the magnitude of his power over Matter) the concern is growing for what I have called "an open Universe," that is for an endless preservation of human conquests.

Most certainly, too, in modern Man (because he has suddenly realized both the fantastic dimensions and the incredible organicity of the physical World) the attraction is more distinctly felt for a Whole and a Oneness no longer conceived or experienced as a dissolving Ocean, but as a mighty focus of unification and of completion.

On the one hand a clarified Sense of the Irreversible; and, on the other, a corrected and generalized sense of the Cosmic or of the Universal . . .

Observing this two-fold change in our mind, I can not help thinking that we are entering a new age, and that, as a consequence, a new field of research is just opening for all those interested in the psychological sciences.

So far (and for good reasons) the psychologists have been concerned principally with the medical task of freeing the individual patients from their hidden or buried "complexes." But now the time has come, for all of them, to attack the engineering work of exploring and tapping the mysterious zones where still lie, untouched, the most powerful energies of the human soul: the sense of the Irreversible, the cosmic sense, the sense of Earth, the human sense . . .

Ultimately there is no other fuel, no other blood, able to feed (and to humanize at the same time) the giant organism built up by human socialization, but a *new type of faith* in the future of the Species and in a spiritual climaxing of the World.

Under such circumstances, and of course without neglecting the material advance of technology, it is towards the increase of our internal *evolutive drive*, it is towards the clarification in ourselves of the *cosmic libido*, that we must devote henceforth the better part of our attention.

Tomorrow, a new "psycho-dynamics" will probably be of more use than our present electro —and thermo—dynamics.

Let us not forget that nowhere are the elements of a complete "evolutive energy" better recognizable and more advanced today than in a well understood Christianity: that is to say, in the flaming perception of a Universe which is neither cold, nor closed—but which irreversibly converges (Matter and Spirit altogether) on a loving and lovable Center of intense personality.

PARIS, 1948

Translated by Joseph L. Caulfield

For Further Reading:

A selection of books by Teilhard de Chardin

THE APPEARANCE OF MAN; New York, Harper & Row, $5.00

THE DIVINE MILIEU: An Essay on the Interior Life; New York, Harper & Row (Harper Torchbook TB384), Paperback, $1.25

THE FUTURE OF MAN; New York, Harper & Row, $5.95

LETTERS FROM A TRAVELER; New York, Harper & Row, $5.00

LETTERS FROM HASTINGS; New York, Herder & Herder, $4.95

THE MAKING OF A MIND; New York, Harper & Row, $5.00

MAN'S PLACE IN NATURE; New York, Harper & Row, $3.50

THE PHENOMENON OF MAN; New York, Harper & Row, $5.95
Also (Harper Torchbook TB383) Paperback, $1.95

SCIENCE AND CHRIST; New York, Harper & Row, $5.00

THE VISION OF THE PAST; New York, Harper & Row, $5.00

WRITINGS IN TIME OF WAR; New York, Harper & Row, $5.95

A selection of books about Teilhard de Chardin

Baltazar, Eulalio R. TEILHARD AND THE SUPERNATURAL; New York, Taplinger, $6.95

Barbour, G. B. IN THE FIELD WITH TEILHARD de CHARDIN; New York, Herder & Herder, $3.95

Bravo, Francisco. CHRIST IN THE THOUGHT OF TEILHARD de CHARDIN; Notre Dame, Ind., University of Notre Dame Press, $4.95

Braybrooke, Neville, ed. TEILHARD de CHARDIN: Pilgrim of the Future; New York, Seabury Press, $3.50

Chauchard, Paul. Man and Cosmos; New York, Herder and Herder, $4.50

Chauchard, Paul. TEILHARD de CHARDIN ON LOVE AND SUFFERING; Glen Rock, N. J., Paulist Press, Paperback, .75

Corte, Nicholas. PIERRE TEILHARD de CHARDIN: His Life and Spirit. tr. by M. Jarrett-Kerr; New York, MacMillan Co., $3.50

Crespy, Georges. FROM SCIENCE TO THEOLOGY. tr. by George H. Shriver; New York and Nashville, Tenn., Abingdon Press, $4.00

Cuénot, Claude. TEILHARD de CHARDIN: A Biographical Study. ed. by R. Hague. tr. by V. Colimore; New York, Taplinger, $9.75

De Lubac, Henri. TEILHARD EXPLAINED; Glen Rock, Paulist Press, Paperback, .95
Devaux, André A. TEILHARD AND WOMANHOOD; Glen Rock, Paulist Press, Paperback, .95
Faricy, Robert. TEILHARD de CHARDIN'S THEOLOGY OF THE CHRISTIAN WORLD; New York, Sheed and Ward, $6.00
Kopp, Joseph. TEILHARD de CHARDIN: New Synthesis of Evolution. 1964, Paulist Press, Paperback, .75
Lepp, Ignace. FAITH OF MEN. tr. by Bernard Murchland. New York, MacMillan Co., $3.95
Ligneul André. TEILHARD AND PERSONALISM; Paulist Press, Paperback, .95
Lubac. TEILHARD de CHARDIN. tr. by R. Hague; New York, Hawthorn, $5.95
Lubac. TEILHARD de CHARDIN: the Man and His Meaning; New York, New American Library, Inc., Paperback, .75
Martin, Maria Gratia. SPIRITUALITY of TEILHARD de CHARDIN; Glen Rock, N. J., Newman Press, $4.95
Mooney, Christopher F. TEILHARD de CHARDIN AND THE MYSTERY OF CHRIST; New York, Harper & Row, $6.00
Murray, Michael H. THOUGHT OF TEILHARD de CHARDIN: An Introduction; New York, Seabury Press, $4.95

Rabut, Oliver. TEILHARD de CHARDIN; New York, Sheed and Ward, $3.95

Raven, Charles E. TEILHARD de CHARDIN; New York, Harper & Row, $4.00

Rideau, Emile. THOUGHT of TEILHARD de CHARDIN; Harper & Row, $12.50

Smulders, Piet. DESIGN OF TEILHARD de CHARDIN; Glen Rock, N. J., Newman Press, $7.50

Speaight, Robert. LIFE OF TEILHARD de CHARDIN; New York, Harper & Row, $8.50

Towers, Bernard. TEILHARD de CHARDIN; Richmond, Va., John Knox Press, Paperback, $1.25

Wildiers, N. M. INTRODUCTION TO TEILHARD de CHARDIN; New York, Harper & Row, $6.00